M000272035

Super Quick
QUILTS

Martingale®
Create with Confidence

Super Quick Quilts

© 2013 by Martingale & Company®

Martingale

19021 120th Ave. NE, Ste. 102
Bothell, WA 98011-9511 USA
ShopMartingale.com

No part of this product may be reproduced in any form, unless otherwise stated, in which case reproduction is limited to the use of the purchaser. The written instructions, photographs, designs, projects, and patterns are intended for the personal, noncommercial use of the retail purchaser and are under federal copyright laws; they are not to be reproduced by any electronic, mechanical, or other means, including informational storage or retrieval systems, for commercial use. Permission is granted to photocopy patterns for the personal use of the retail purchaser. Attention teachers: Martingale encourages you to use this book for teaching, subject to the restrictions stated above.

The information in this book is presented in good faith, but no warranty is given nor results guaranteed. Since Martingale has no control over choice of materials or procedures, the company assumes no responsibility for the use of this information.

Printed in China
18 17 16 15 14 13   8 7 6 5 4 3 2

Library of Congress Cataloging-in-Publication Data is available upon request.
ISBN: 978-1-60468-341-7

Mission Statement

Dedicated to providing quality products
and service to inspire creativity.

What's your creative passion?
Find it at ShopMartingale.com
books • eBooks • ePatterns • daily blog • free projects
videos • tutorials • inspiration • giveaways

Contents

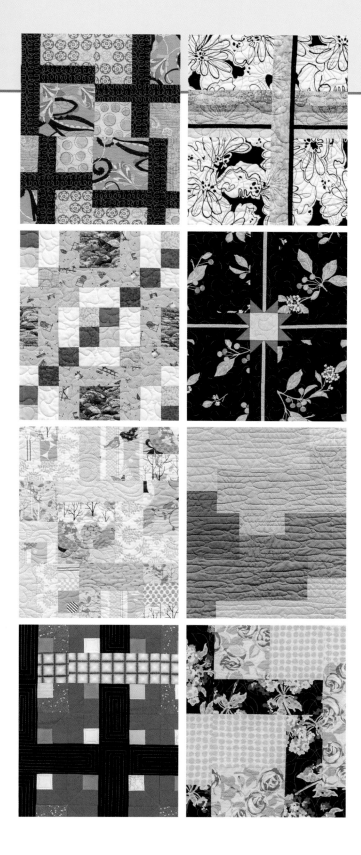

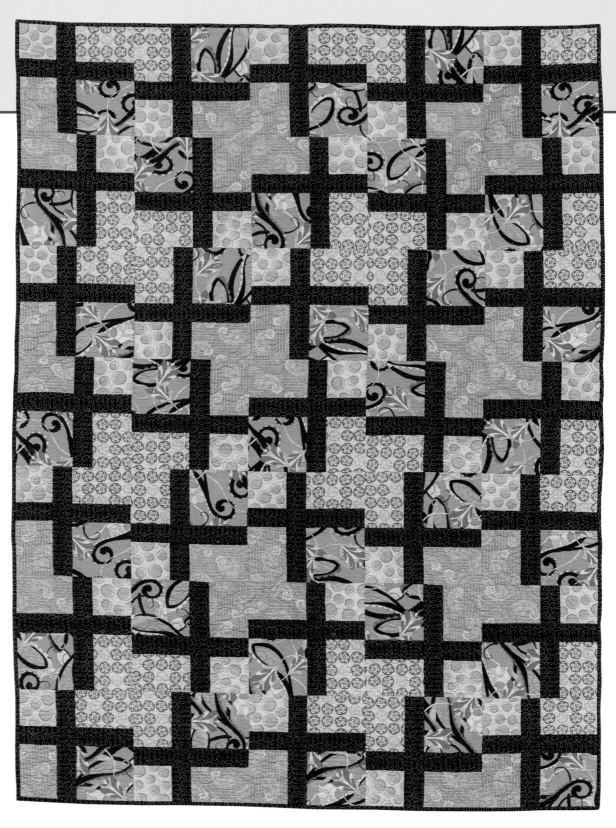

Designed and pieced by Amy Ellis; machine quilted by Natalia Bonner

Quilt size: 60" x 84" • **Block size:** 12" x 12"

Modern Maze

This quilt is a fun way to show off some of your favorite fabrics—each has a turn being the star of your quilt!

Materials

Yardage is based on 42"-wide fabrics.

2 yards of brown print for blocks and binding
1¼ yards of pink print for blocks
1⅛ yards of green print for blocks
⅞ yard of cream print for blocks
¾ yard of cream-with-green-dots print for blocks
5 yards of fabric for backing
66" x 90" piece of batting

Cutting

All measurements include ¼"-wide seam allowances.
Cut all strips across the width of the fabric.

From the cream-with-green-dots print, cut:
5 strips, 4" x 42"

From the brown print, cut:
31 strips, 2" x 42"; crosscut 12 of the strips into
   35 rectangles, 2" x 12"

From the green print, cut:
5 strips, 6" x 42"

From the cream print, cut:
6 strips, 4" x 42"

From the pink print, cut:
6 strips, 6" x 42"

Piecing the Blocks

1. Pin and sew a cream-with-green-dots strip, a brown strip, and a green strip together. Press the seam allowances toward the brown strips. Make five strip sets. Cut the strip sets into 35 segments, 4½" wide.

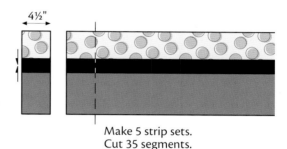

4½"

Make 5 strip sets.
Cut 35 segments.

2. Pin and sew a cream strip, a brown strip, and a pink strip together. Press the seam allowances toward the brown strip. Make six strip sets. Cut the strip sets into 35 segments, 6½" wide.

6½"

Make 6 strip sets.
Cut 35 segments.

3 Pin and sew a 4½"-wide segment from step 1, a brown rectangle, and a 6½"-wide segment from step 2 together as shown. Press the seam allowances toward the brown rectangle. Make 35 blocks. Trim and square the blocks to 12½" x 12½".

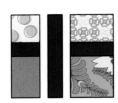 

Make 35.

Assembling the Quilt Top

1 Lay out seven rows of five blocks each, orienting the blocks as shown. Pin and sew the blocks together in rows, pressing the seam allowances in alternate directions from row to row.

2 Sew the rows together to complete the quilt top. Press the seam allowances in one direction.

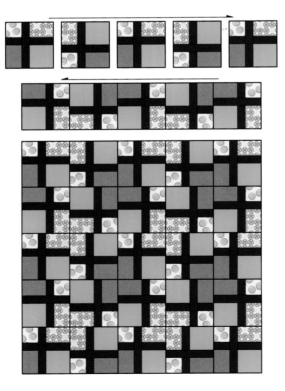

Finishing the Quilt

Go to ShopMartingale.com/HowtoQuilt for more information on finishing your quilt.

1 Cut the length of the backing fabric in half to create two 90"-long pieces. Sew the two pieces together side by side and press the seam allowances open.

2 Layer the backing, batting, and quilt top; baste. Quilt as desired.

3 Bind the edges of the quilt using the remaining brown 2½"-wide strips.

Simple Strips

Find a black-and-white print that you love, add a few bright colors, and you're ready to make this easy strip-pieced quilt.

Materials

Yardage is based on 42"-wide fabric.

3⅛ yards of black-and-white floral print for quilt center and border 4

⅛ yard *each* of 6 assorted bright prints for quilt center

⅔ yard of green-and-teal print for quilt center and binding

½ yard of green-and-blue-dot print for quilt center and border 3

⅜ yard of black-dot print for quilt center and border 2

⅓ yard of green-swirl print for quilt center and border 1

¼ yard of bright-purple print for quilt center

¼ yard of bright-yellow batik for quilt center

4 yards of fabric for backing

68" x 88" piece of batting

Cutting

All measurements include ¼"-wide seam allowances. Cut all strips across the width of the fabric.

From the bright-purple print, cut:
1 strip, 2¼" x 42"
1 strip, 2" x 42"

From the 6 bright prints, cut:
1 strip, 1¼" x 42" (green vine)
1 strip, 1½" x 42" (green vine)
1 strip, 1½" x 42" (yellow dot)
1 strip, 2" x 42" (green dot)
1 strip, 1¾" x 42" (red plaid)
2 strips, 1½" x 42" (blue dot)
1 strip, 1¾" x 42" (orange)

From the green-and-blue-dot print, cut:
1 strip, 2" x 42"
6 strips, 1¾" x 42"

From the black-dot print, cut:
9 strips, 1" x 42"
1 strip, 1¼" x 42"

From the black-and-white floral print, cut:
1 strip, 8" x 42"; crosscut into 1 piece, 8" x 11½", and 1 piece, 8" x 25"
1 strip, 11" x 42"; crosscut into 1 piece, 11" x 11½", and 1 piece, 11" x 25"
1 strip, 13½" x 42"; crosscut into 1 piece, 13½" x 38½"
1 strip, 9" x 42"; crosscut into 1 piece, 9" x 38½"
7 strips, 8½" x 42"

From the green-swirl print, cut:
6 strips, 1½" x 42"

From the bright-yellow batik, cut:
1 strip, 1½" x 42"
1 strip, 2" x 42"

From the green-and-teal print, cut:
1 strip, 2" x 42"
8 strips, 2¼" x 42"

Making the Blocks

1 Sew the bright-purple 2¼" strip, the green-vine 1¼" strip, the green-and-blue-dot 2" strip, a black-dot 1" strip, and the yellow-dot 1½" strip together. Press the seam allowances in one direction. Cut the strip set into one segment, 11½" wide, and one segment, 25" wide.

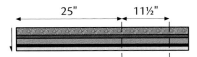

2 Sew the black-and-white floral 8" x 11½" and 8" x 25" pieces to the top of the strip-set segments. Sew the black-and-white floral 11" x 11½" and 11" x 25" pieces to the bottom of the strip-set segments. Press the seam allowances toward the strips.

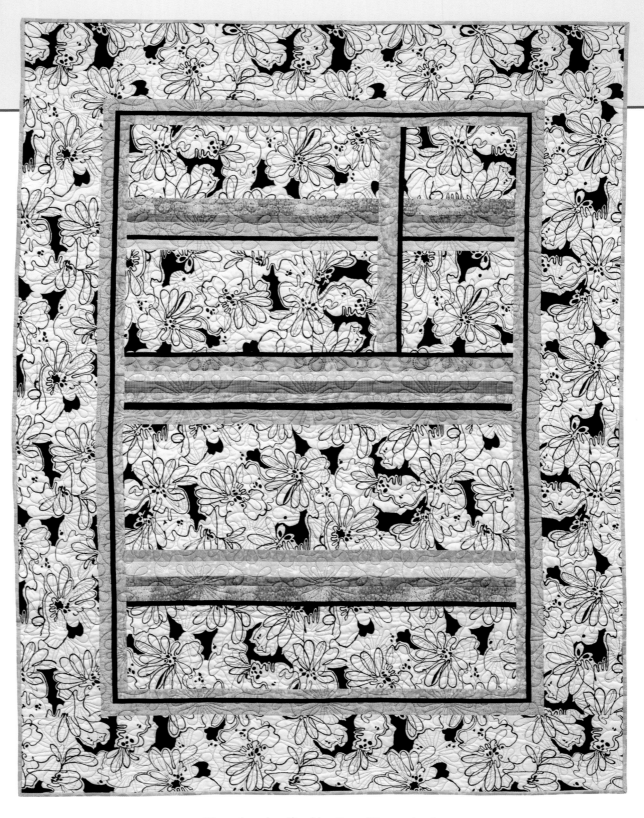

Pieced and quilted by Sara Diepersloot

Quilt size: 60" x 80½"

3 Sew a black-dot 1" strip, a green-swirl 1½" strip, and a blue-dot 1½" strip together. Press the seam allowances in one direction. Cut the strip set into one segment, 24" wide.

4 Sew the 24" strip-set segment between the 25" strip set and the 11½" strip set. Press the seam allowances toward the center.

5 Sew a black-dot 1" strip, the green-dot 2" strip, the yellow-batik 1½" strip, the red-plaid 1¾" strip, the remaining blue-dot 1½" strip, the black-dot 1¼" strip, and the green-and-teal print 2" strip together. Press the seam allowances in one direction. Cut the strip set into one segment, 38½" wide.

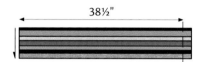

6 Sew the black-and-white floral 13½" x 38½" piece to the bottom of the strip-set segment. Press toward the strips.

7 Sew the orange 1¾" strip, the yellow-batik 2" strip, the green-vine 1½" strip, the bright-purple 2" strip, and a black-dot 1" strip together. Press the seam allowances in one direction. Cut the strip set into one segment, 38½" wide.

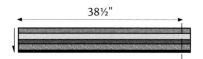

8 Sew the black-and-white floral 9" x 38½" piece to the bottom of the strip-set segment. Press the seam allowances toward the strips.

Assembling the Quilt Top

1 Sew the strip-pieced units together as shown in the quilt diagram below.

2 Attach the four borders in this order: green swirl, black dot, green-and-blue dot, and black-and-white floral.

Finishing the Quilt

Go to ShopMartingale.com/HowtoQuilt for more information on finishing your quilt.

1 Layer the quilt top with batting and backing; baste. Quilt as desired.

2 Bind the edges of the quilt using the green-and-teal strips.

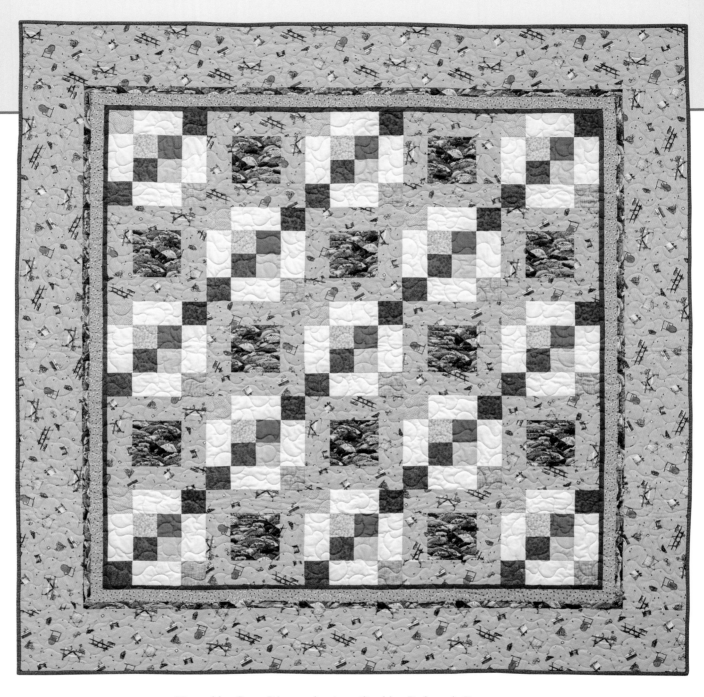

Pieced by Sara Diepersloot; quilted by Deborah Rasmussen

Quilt size: 68½" x 68½" • **Block size:** 10" x 10"

Campout

Whip up this quilt and take it on your next picnic. Or cuddle up at the campfire, and then layer it over your sleeping bag when it's time to hit the sack.

Materials

Yardage is based on 42"-wide fabric.

2½ yards of small-scale green camping print for blocks and border 4

⅞ yard of white fabric for blocks

⅝ yard of large-scale green camping print for blocks and border 3

⅛ yard *each* of 4 different red fabrics for blocks

⅛ yard *each* of 4 different green fabrics for blocks

⅜ yard of green bee print for border 2

¼ yard of red print for border 1

⅝ yard of red print for binding

4½ yards of fabric for backing

77" x 77" piece of batting

Cutting

All measurements include ¼"-wide seam allowances. Cut all strips across the width of the fabric.

From *each* of the 4 different red fabrics, cut:
1 strip, 3" x 42" (4 total)

From *each* of the 4 different green fabrics, cut:
1 strip, 3" x 42" (4 total)

From the white fabric, cut:
8 strips, 3" x 42"; crosscut into 52 rectangles, 3" x 5½"

From the small-scale green camping print, cut:
11 strips, 3" x 42"; crosscut into 24 rectangles, 3" x 5½", and 24 rectangles, 3" x 10½"
7 strips, 7" x 42"

From the large-scale green camping print, cut:
2 strips, 5½" x 42"; crosscut into 12 squares, 5½" x 5½"
6 strips, 1¼" x 42"

From the red print for border 1, cut:
6 strips, 1" x 42"

From the green bee print, cut:
6 strips, 1¾" x 42"

From the red print for binding, cut:
8 strips, 2¼" x 40"

Making Block A

1 From the red and green 3" x 42" strips, choose the two red fabrics and two green fabrics you want to have in the center four-patch unit of the blocks. Sew one red strip to one green strip to make a strip set. Press the seam allowances toward the red strip. Repeat with the second red and green strips to make two strip sets. Crosscut each strip set into 13 segments, 3" wide.

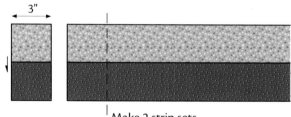

3"

Make 2 strip sets.
Cut 26 segments total.

2 Sew 3" segments together to make a four-patch unit. Press. Make 13 units.

Make 13.

3 Cut the remaining red and green 3" x 42" strips into 3" squares. You'll need 13 of each color.

4 Sew a red and a green 3" square to opposite ends of a white 3" x 5½" rectangle. Press the seam allowances toward the corner squares. Make 26.

Make 26.

5 Sew 3" x 5½" white rectangles to opposite sides of a four-patch unit. Press the seam allowances toward the four-patch unit.

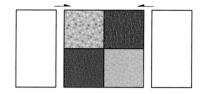

6 Join the segments from steps 4 and 5 to make block A. Make 13 of block A.

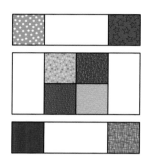 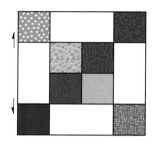

Make 13.

Making Block B

1 Sew small-scale camping print 3" x 5½" rectangles to opposite sides of a large-scale camping print 5½" square. Press.

2 Sew small-scale 3" x 10½" rectangle to the top and bottom of the center unit. Press the seam allowances away from the center square. Repeat to make 12 of block B.

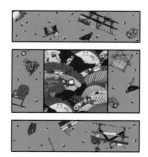 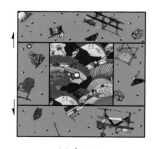

Make 12.

Assembling the Quilt Top

1 Arrange the A and B blocks together into five rows of five blocks each, alternating the A and B blocks. Press the seam allowances toward the B blocks. Join the rows. Press the seam allowances in one direction.

2 Attach the four borders in this order: red print, green bee print, large-scale green camping print, and small-scale green camping print.

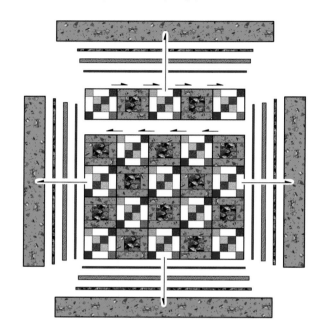

Finishing the Quilt

Go to ShopMartingale.com/HowtoQuilt for more information on finishing your quilt.

1 Layer the quilt top with batting and backing; baste. Quilt as desired.

2 Bind the edges of the quilt using the red strips.

Cherry Blossoms

Large squares are the perfect way to showcase a fabulous print, such as this beautiful black print that was a tablecloth in its first life.

Materials

Yardage is based on 42"-wide fabric.

3¾ yards of black cherry-blossom print for blocks

1⅔ yards of black-dot print for sashing

1⅜ yard of red fabric for star points and binding

½ yard of green fabric for sashing

⅓ yard of yellow fabric for star centers

4⅓ yards of fabric for backing

79" x 79" piece of batting

Cutting

All measurements include ¼"-wide seam allowances. Cut all strips across the width of the fabric.

From the black-dot print, cut:
24 strips, 2¼" x 42"

From the green fabric, cut:
12 strips, 1" x 42"

From the red fabric, cut:
8 strips, 2½" x 42"; crosscut into 128 squares, 2½" x 2½"
8 strips, 2¼" x 42"

From the black cherry-blossom print, cut:
5 strips, 16½" x 42"; crosscut into 9 squares, 16½" x 16½"
8 strips, 4½" x 42"; crosscut into 20 squares, 4½" x 4½", and 12 rectangles, 4½" x 16½"

From the yellow fabric, cut:
2 strips, 4½" x 42"; crosscut into 16 squares, 4½" x 4½"

Making the Sashing Units

1 Sew a black-dot strip, a green strip, and another black-dot strip together to make a strip set. Make 12 strip sets. Press the seam allowances toward the black. Cut each strip set into two segments, 4½" x 16½", for a total of 24 segments.

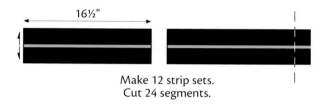

Make 12 strip sets.
Cut 24 segments.

2 Mark a diagonal line on the wrong side of each red square. Lay a red square on the end of a segment from step 1, right sides together, and sew on the diagonal line as shown. Trim off the excess about ¼" from the sewn line. Press the seam allowances toward the red star point.

3 Repeat step 2 to add a red star point to each corner. Make 24 sashing units.

Make 24.

4 Using the remaining red squares, add red triangles to two corners of a cherry-blossom 4½" square as shown to make star points for the borders. Make 16 star-point units.

Make 16.

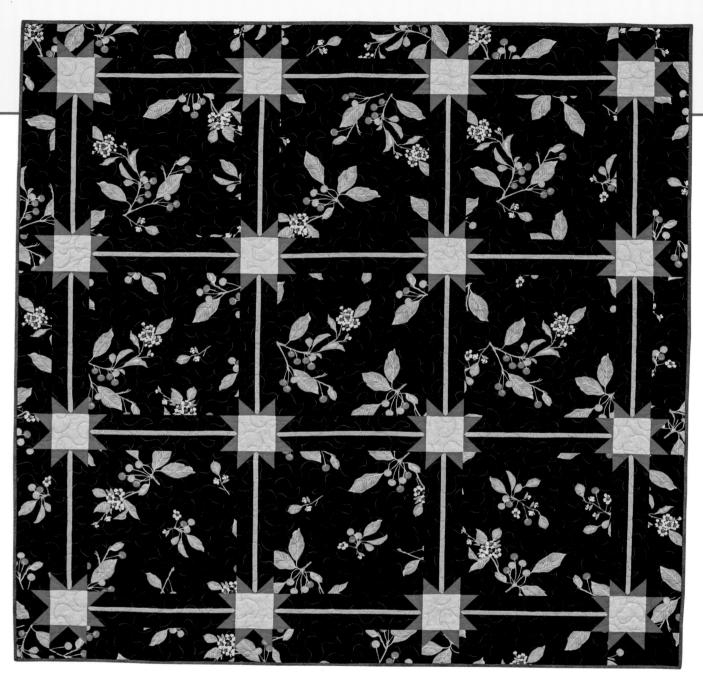

Pieced by Sara Diepersloot, quilted by Deborah Rasmussen

Quilt size: 72½" x 72½"

Assembling the Quilt Top

The quilt top consists of three different rows.

1 For row 1, join two of the remaining cherry-blossom 4½" squares, four star-point units from step 4 of "Making the Sashing Units" on page 13, and three cherry-blossom 4½" x 16½" rectangles as shown. Press the seam allowances toward the cherry-blossom print. Make two rows.

Row 1
Make 2.

2 For row 2, join two star-point units, four yellow squares, and three sashing units as shown. Press the seam allowances toward the yellow squares. Make four rows.

Row 2.
Make 4.

3 For row 3, join two cherry-blossom 4½" x 16½" rectangles, four sashing units, and three cherry-blossom 16½" squares as shown. Press the seam allowances toward the cherry-blossom print. Make three rows.

Row 3.
Make 3.

4 Join the rows as shown. Press.

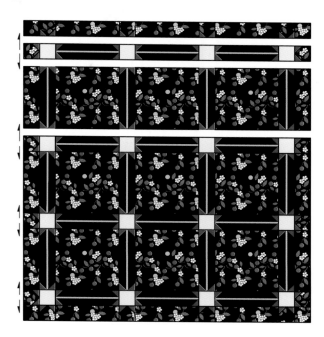

Finishing the Quilt

Go to ShopMartingale.com/HowtoQuilt for more information on finishing your quilt.

1 Layer the quilt top with batting and backing; baste. Quilt as desired.

2 Bind the edges of the quilt using the red strips.

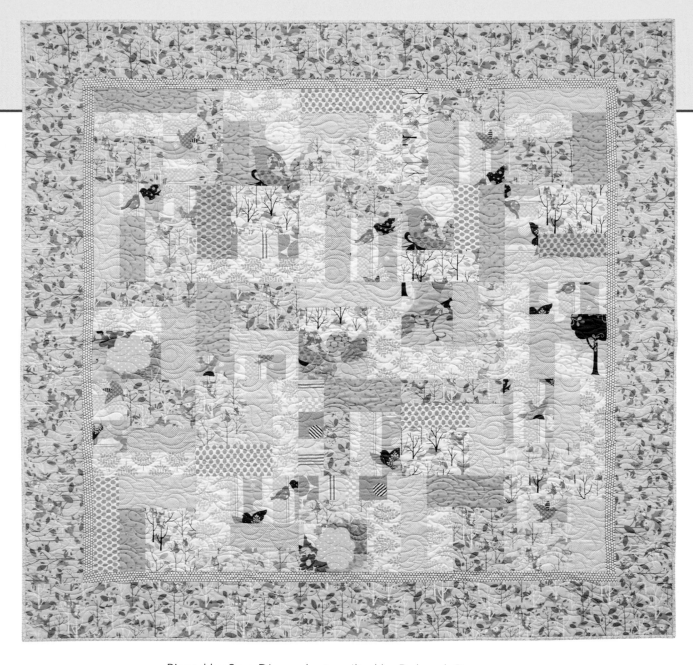

Pieced by Sara Diepersloot; quilted by Deborah Rasmussen

Quilt size: 76" x 76" • **Block size:** 12" x 12"

Nest

These super-easy blocks are pieced like Half Log Cabin blocks. Their large size allows the fabrics to shine.

Materials

Yardage is based on 42"-wide fabric.

4 yards *total* of assorted prints for blocks*
2 yards of aqua print for blocks and outer border
½ yard of pink polka-dot print for inner border
⅝ yard of pink print for binding
4¾ yards of fabric for backing
84" x 84" piece of batting

*This quilt uses ½-yard cuts of 12 fabrics to allow enough to fussy cut pieces.

Cutting

All measurements include ¼"-wide seam allowances.
Cut all strips across the width of the fabric.

From the aqua print, cut:
7 strips, 7" x 42"

From the assorted prints and remainder of aqua print, cut a *total* of:
25 pieces, 6½" x 8½"
25 pieces, 3½" x 8½"
25 pieces, 3½" x 12½"
25 pieces, 4½" x 9½"

From the pink polka-dot print, cut:
7 strips, 1¾" x 42"

From the pink print, cut:
8 strips, 2¼" x 42"

Making the Blocks

Cut out the blocks one at a time and decide which fabrics you want next to each other. When using directional fabrics, take care to orient the cutting correctly. This is a great time to use a design wall.

1 Sew a 3½" x 8½" rectangle to a 6½" x 8½" rectangle as shown. Press the seam allowances toward the smaller rectangle.

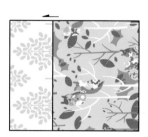

2 Sew a 4½" x 9½" rectangle to the top of the unit made in step 1. Press the seam allowances toward the rectangle just added.

3 Sew a 3½" x 12½" rectangle to the left side of the unit made in step 2. Press toward the rectangle just added.

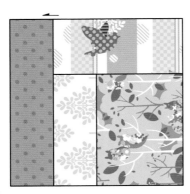

4 Repeat steps 1–3 to make 25 blocks.

Assembling the Quilt Top

1 Arrange the blocks in five rows of five blocks each as shown in the quilt diagram at right, rotating the blocks as desired.

2 Join the blocks into rows. Press the seam allowances in opposite directions from row to row. Sew the rows together. Press the seam allowances in one direction.

3 Attach the pink polka-dot inner and aqua-print outer borders.

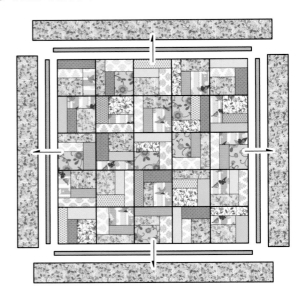

Finishing the Quilt

Go to ShopMartingale.com/HowtoQuilt for more information on finishing your quilt.

1 Layer the quilt top with batting and backing; baste. Quilt as desired.

2 Bind the edges of the quilt using the pink strips.

Basic Puzzle

This quilt is made without blocks; instead there are three different rows that repeat in a variety of colors.

Materials

Yardage is based on 42"-wide fabrics.

⅓ yard *each* of 12 assorted solids
½ yard of white solid for binding
3¾ yards of fabric for backing
56" x 66" piece of batting

Cutting

All measurements include ¼"-wide seam allowances. Cut all strips across the width of the fabric. The number of pieces cut are more than you will need for your quilt. This is to ensure that you can arrange the colors as you like. You can use the leftovers on the back of your quilt or for another project.

From *each* of the 12 solids, cut:
2 strips, 4½" x 42"; crosscut into:
    4 rectangles, 4½" x 14½" (48 total)
    8 rectangles, 2½" x 4½" (96 total)

From the white solid, cut:
6 binding strips, 2½" x 42"

Assembling the Quilt Top

With no blocks to assemble, this quilt top can be sewn without delay! As this quilt is a bit of a puzzle, it's best to use a design wall to arrange the pieces for the quilt. Start by laying out all of the large rectangles randomly for steps 1, 2, and 3 until you find a pleasing arrangement of colors. Follow the directions for adding small rectangles and for piecing the first three rows to make all the rows in the quilt.

1 For the first row, arrange three large rectangles and four small rectangles as shown. Pin and sew the pairs of small rectangles together on the long sides, and then sew them between the large rectangles. Press the seam allowances open.

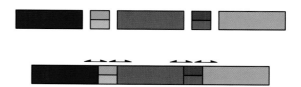

2 For the second row, select three large rectangles and six small rectangles, matching the rectangles to the row above and below as shown. Cut the far-right rectangle into two pieces measuring 4½" x 8½" and 2½" x 4½". Arrange the pieces as shown. Pin and sew the small rectangles together first; then sew the row together. Press the seam allowances open.

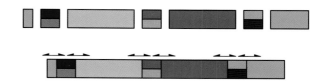

3 For the third row, select three large rectangles and six small rectangles, matching the rectangles to the row above and below as shown. Cut the far-left rectangle into two pieces measuring 4½" x 8½" and 2½" x 4½". Arrange the pieces as shown. Pin and sew the small rectangles together first; then sew the row together. Press the seam allowances open.

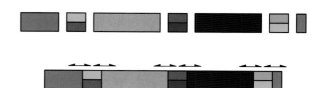

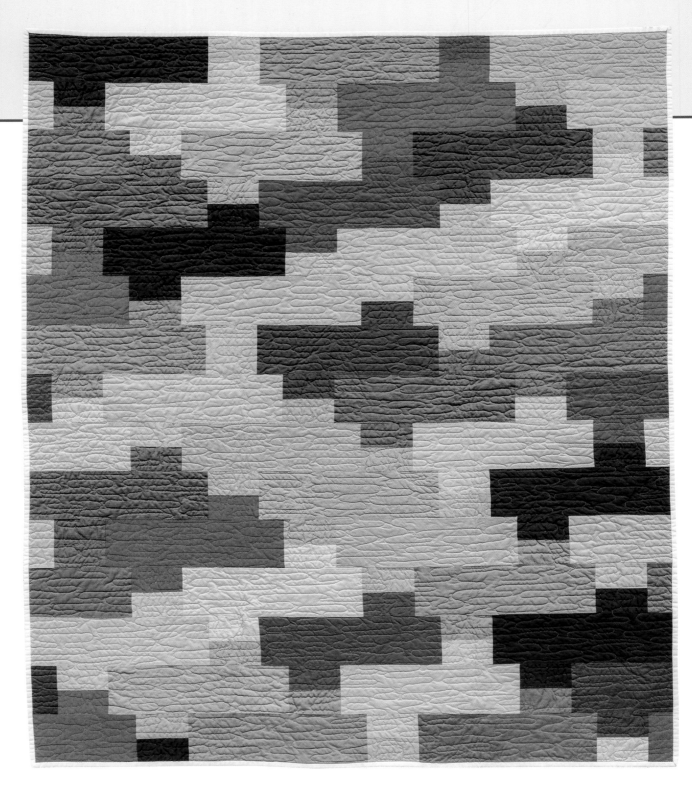

Designed and pieced by Amy Ellis; quilted by Natalia Bonner

Quilt size: 50½" x 60½"

4 Sew the first, second, and third rows together. Press the seam allowances open.

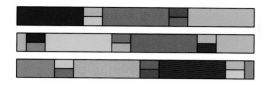

5 Repeat steps 1 through 4 to make a *total* of 15 rows; sew the rows in groups of three to make larger rows. Be sure to match large and small rectangles to the colors in previous rows. Press the seam allowances open.

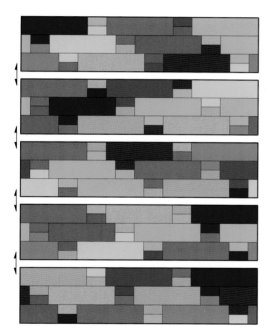

Finishing the Quilt

Go to ShopMartingale.com/HowtoQuilt for more information on finishing your quilt.

1 Layer the quilt top with batting and backing; baste. Quilt as desired.

2 Bind the edges of the quilt using the white strips.

By Julie Popa; quilted by Paula Murray

Quilt size: 57½" x 69½" • **Block size:** 12" x 12"

City Streets

This quilt makes a great gift for a son, grandson, or other special guy in your life. The simple design makes the project easy to complete in a weekend.

Materials

Yardage is based on 42"-wide fabric.

2⅓ yards of black print for blocks and border
1 yard of blue solid for blocks
½ yard of blue print for blocks
⅝ yard *total* of assorted red, yellow, and white solids
   for blocks
⅝ yard of gray print for blocks
⅝ yard of black-and-white print for binding
4 yards of fabric for backing
65" x 77" piece of batting

Cutting

All measurements include ¼"-wide seam allowances.
Cut all strips across the width of the fabric.

From the assorted red, yellow, and white solids, cut a *total* of:
80 squares, 2½" x 2½"

From the blue solid, cut:
56 squares, 2½" x 2½"
56 rectangles, 2½" x 4½"

From the blue print, cut:
24 squares, 2½" x 2½"
24 rectangles, 2½" x 4½"

From the black print, cut:
14 rectangles, 4½" x 12½"
28 squares, 4½" x 4½"
7 strips, 5" x 42"

From the gray print, cut:
6 rectangles, 4½" x 12½"
12 squares, 4½" x 4½"

From the black-and-white print, cut:
7 strips, 2½" x 42"

Making the Blocks

1 Sew each of the assorted red, yellow, and white 2½" squares to a blue-solid or blue-print 2½" square. Make a total of 80 units. Press the seam allowances toward the blue squares.

Make 56.   Make 24.

2 Sew the blue-solid 2½" x 4½" rectangles to each unit from step 1 that has a blue-solid square as shown. Repeat with the blue-print rectangles and the remaining step 1 units. Press the seam allowances toward the rectangles.

Make 56.   Make 24.

3 Sew the step 2 units and the black and gray 4½" squares together as shown. Make the number of units indicated for each color combination. Press the seam allowances toward the squares.

 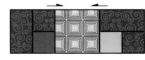

Make 28.   Make 12.

4 Sew the step 3 units to the long edges of the black and gray 4½" x 12½" rectangles. Make the number indicated for each color combination. Press the seam allowances toward the rectangles.

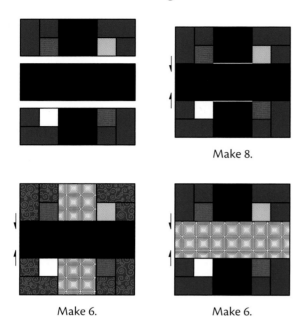

Make 8.

Make 6.   Make 6.

Assembling the Quilt Top

1 Arrange the blocks in five horizontal rows of four blocks each as shown. Be careful to place the correct block in each position, rotating it as needed. Sew the blocks into rows. Press the seam allowances

in opposite directions from row to row. Sew the rows together. Press the seam allowances in one direction.

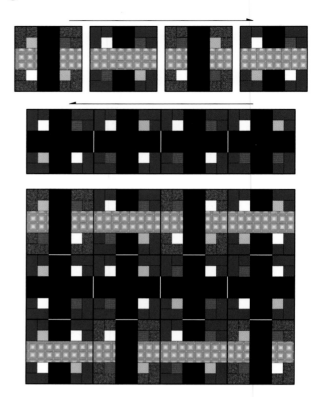

2 Sew the black 5" x 42" strips together end to end and press the seam allowances to one side. Measure the length of your quilt; then cut and sew the black borders. After attaching the side borders, repeat for the top and bottom border.

Finishing the Quilt

Go to ShopMartingale.com/HowtoQuilt for more information on finishing your quilt.

1 Layer the quilt top with batting and backing; baste. Quilt as desired.

2 Bind the edges of the quilt using the black-and-white strips.

Modern Mirrors

This full-sized quilt is assembled from simple blocks. The challenge is in putting all the pieces together, but give yourself plenty of space to lay out all the blocks and the results will be striking!

Materials

Yardage is based on 42"-wide fabric.

3¼ yards of aqua print for blocks
3 yards of brown solid for blocks
36 assorted strips, 2½" x 42", for blocks
¾ yard of pink print for binding
6¾ yards of fabric for backing
88" x 96" piece of batting

Cutting

All measurements include ¼"-wide seam allowances.
Cut all strips across the width of the fabric.

From the aqua print, cut:
36 strips, 2½" x 42"; crosscut 18 of the strips into:
    60 rectangles, 2½" x 8½"
    30 rectangles, 2½" x 10½"

From the brown solid, cut:
30 strips, 2½" x 42"; crosscut 12 of the strips into:
    48 rectangles, 2½" x 8½"
    24 rectangles, 2½" x 10½"

From the pink print, cut:
9 strips, 2½" x 42"

Piecing the Blocks

1 Pin and sew together four assorted strips to make a strip set. Press the seam allowances in one direction. Make nine strip sets. Cut the strip sets into 54 center segments, 6½" wide.

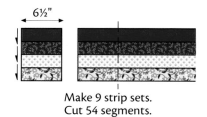

Make 9 strip sets.
Cut 54 segments.

2 Pin and sew an aqua 2½" x 8½" rectangle to a center segment as shown. Pin and sew a brown 2½" x 8½" rectangle to another center segment as shown. Press the seam allowances toward the rectangles just added. Make 30 aqua units and 24 brown units.

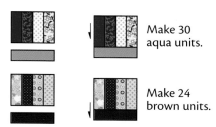

Make 30 aqua units.

Make 24 brown units.

3 Pin and sew an aqua 2½" x 8½" rectangle to the left side of an aqua unit and a brown 2½" x 8½" rectangle to the left side of a brown unit. Press the seam allowances toward the rectangles just added. Make 30 aqua units and 24 brown units.

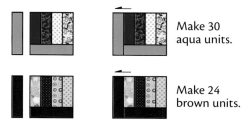

Make 30 aqua units.

Make 24 brown units.

4 Pin and sew an aqua 2½" x 10½" rectangle to the top of an aqua unit. Pin and sew a brown 2½" x 10½" rectangle to the top of a brown unit. Press the seam allowances toward the rectangles just added. Make 30 aqua units and 24 brown units.

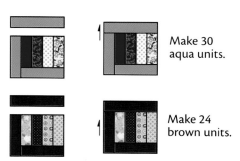

Make 30 aqua units.

Make 24 brown units.

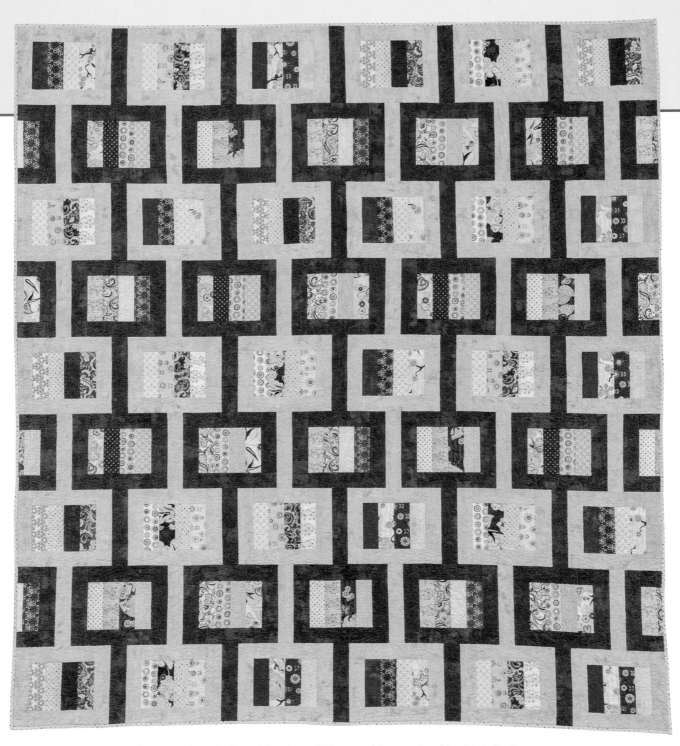

Designed and pieced by Amy Ellis; machine quilted by Natalia Bonner

Quilt size: 82½" x 90½" • **Block size:** 10" x 14"

5 Pin and sew an aqua 2½"-wide strip to a brown strip to make a strip set. Press the seam allowances toward the brown fabric. Make 18 strip sets. Cut the strip sets from step 6 into 54 segments, 10½" wide.

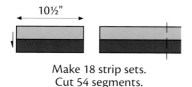

Make 18 strip sets.
Cut 54 segments.

6 Pin and sew the 10½" segments from step 5 to the right-hand side of the units from step 4, placing the appropriate-colored strip next to the block to match the aqua or brown unit. Press the seam allowances toward the rectangles just added. Make 30 aqua blocks and 24 brown blocks. Trim the blocks to 10½" x 14½".

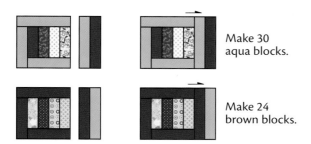

Make 30 aqua blocks.

Make 24 brown blocks.

Assembling the Quilt Top

1 Lay out six aqua blocks in a row. Pin and sew the blocks together. Press the seam allowances toward the right. Undo the stitching and remove the last brown strip at the right-hand end of the row. The row should measure 82½". Make five aqua rows.

Remove last brown strip.

Make 5 aqua rows.

2 Cut four brown blocks between the second and third strips of the four assorted strips as shown; the right piece is one strip wider than the left piece.

3 Lay out a brown row as shown, with the half blocks placed on either end. Pin and sew the blocks together. Press the seam allowances toward the left. Cut 1" from each end of the row to compensate for the brown strip that was removed in step 1. The row should measure 82½". Repeat to make four brown rows.

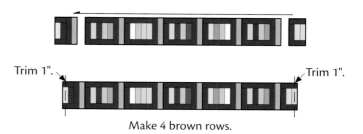

Trim 1".   Trim 1".

Make 4 brown rows.

4 Lay out the rows, alternating aqua and brown rows as shown. Pin and sew the rows together. Press the seam allowances in one direction.

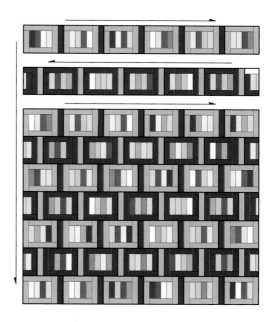

Finishing the Quilt

Go to ShopMartingale.com/HowtoQuilt for more information on finishing your quilt.

1 Layer the quilt top with batting and backing; baste. Quilt as desired.

2 Bind the edges of the quilt using the pink-print strips.

Designed and pieced by Amy Ellis; machine quilted by Natalia Bonner

Quilt size: 60½" x 72½" • **Block size:** 12" x 12"

Basic Ease

This quilt is simple yet interesting, and it's a great project to ease you into quilting. Find beautiful fabrics and sew this quilt, learning as you go!

Materials

Yardage is based on 42"-wide fabric.

1⅝ yards of cream-with-blue-dots print for blocks
1⅝ yards of medium-blue floral for blocks
1⅜ yards of dark-blue floral for blocks
⅝ yard of pink-and-red print for binding
4½ yards of fabric for backing
66" x 78" piece of batting

Cutting

All measurements include ¼"-wide seam allowances. Cut all strips across the width of the fabric.

From the cream-with-blue-dots print, cut:
8 strips, 6½" x 42"

From the medium-blue floral, cut:
8 strips, 6½" x 42"

From the dark-blue floral, cut:
10 strips, 4½" x 42"; crosscut into 30 rectangles, 4½" x 12½"

From the pink-and-red print, cut:
7 binding strips, 2½" x 42"

Piecing the Blocks

1 Pin and sew a cream-with-blue-dots strip to a medium-blue floral strip. Press the seam allowances toward the medium-blue floral. Make eight strip sets. Cut the strip sets into 30 segments, 8½" wide.

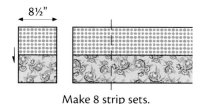

Make 8 strip sets.
Cut 30 segments.

2 Pin and sew a dark-blue floral rectangle to the right side of a segment from step 1. Press the

seam allowances toward the dark blue floral rectangle. Repeat to make 30 blocks. Trim and square the blocks to 12½" x 12½".

Make 30 blocks.

Assembling the Quilt Top

1 Lay out six rows of five blocks each, orienting the blocks as shown. Pin and sew the blocks together in rows, pressing the seam allowances in alternate directions from row to row.

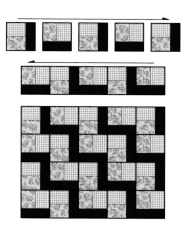

2 Pin and sew the rows together to complete the quilt top. Press the seam allowances in one direction.

Finishing the Quilt

Go to ShopMartingale.com/HowtoQuilt for more information on finishing your quilt.

1 Layer the quilt top with batting and backing; baste. Quilt as desired.

2 Bind the edges of the quilt using the pink-and-red strips.

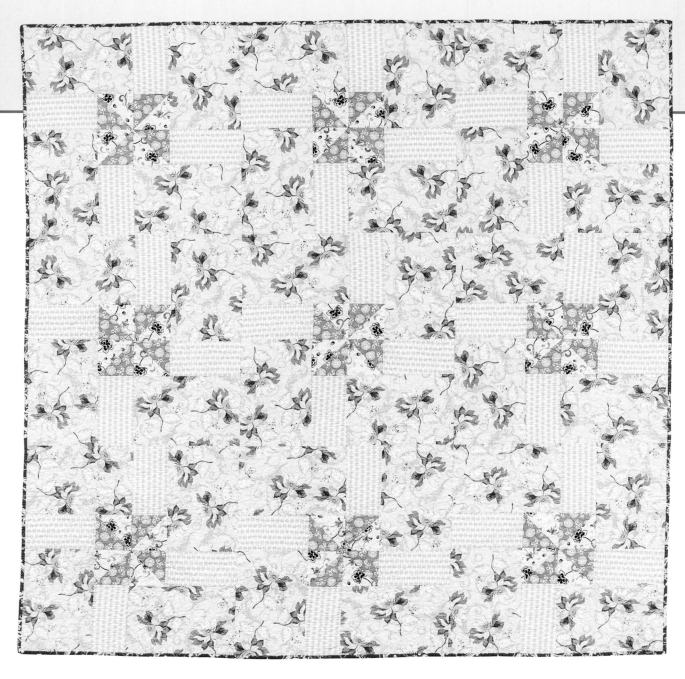

Designed and pieced by Amy Ellis; machine quilted by Natalia Bonner

Quilt size: 72½" x 72½" • **Block size:** 12" x 12"

Wind Power

This quilt introduces a traditional method for making half-square triangles. Once this method is mastered, the options for quilt designs are many!

Materials

Yardage is based on 42"-wide fabric.

3¼ yards of aqua print for blocks
1⅓ yards of pink print for blocks
½ yard of white print for blocks
½ yard of teal print for blocks
⅔ yard of fuchsia print for binding
4½ yards of fabric for backing
78" x 78" piece of batting

Cutting

All measurements include ¼"-wide seam allowances. Cut all strips across the width of the fabric.

From the aqua print, cut:
12 strips, 8½" x 42"; crosscut into 36 rectangles, 8½" x 12½"

From the pink print, cut:
9 strips, 4½" x 42"; crosscut into 36 rectangles, 4½" x 8½"

From the white print, cut:
3 strips, 5" x 42"; crosscut into 18 squares, 5" x 5"

From the teal print, cut:
3 strips, 5" x 42"; crosscut into 18 squares, 5" x 5"

From the fuchsia print, cut:
8 strips, 2½" x 42"

Piecing the Blocks

1 Mark a diagonal line on the wrong side of the 18 white 5" squares.

Mark 18 squares.

2 Pin a white square on top of a teal square. Sew ¼" away from both sides of the drawn line. Repeat with the rest of the pairs of white and teal squares.

Sew 18 pairs.

3 Cut along the marked diagonal line to create two half-square-triangle units. Press the seam allowances open. Make 36 half-square-triangle units.

Cut to make 36
half-square-triangle units.

4 Trim the units to 4½" x 4½". Depending on your seam allowance, you may or may not need to trim off much.

5 Pin and sew a pink rectangle to a half-square-triangle unit. Press the seam allowances toward the pink rectangle. Make 36 units.

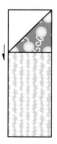

Make 36.

6 Pin and sew an aqua rectangle to the unit from step 5. Press the seam allowances toward the aqua rectangle. Make 36 blocks. Trim and square the blocks to 12½" x 12½".

Make 36.

Assembling the Quilt Top

1 Lay out six rows of six blocks each, orienting the blocks as shown. Pin and sew the blocks together in rows, taking care to match the seams in your pinwheels. Press the seam allowances in alternate directions from row to row.

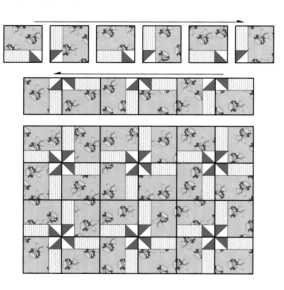

2 Pin and sew the rows together to complete the quilt top. Press the seam allowances in one direction.

Finishing the Quilt

Go to ShopMartingale.com/HowtoQuilt for more information on finishing your quilt.

1 Layer the quilt top with batting and backing; baste. Quilt as desired.

2 Bind the edges of the quilt using the fuchsia strips.